Finding Your Soul Mate in the

FACES OF L♥VE

A Collection of Photographs
With Couples Who Have Similar Facial Features

Christina Bloom

Rutledge Books, Inc. Danbury, CT

ALL RIGHTS RESERVED
Rutledge Books, Inc.
107 Mill Plain Road, Danbury, CT 06811
1-800-278-8533
www.rutledgebooks.com

Manufactured in the United States of America

Cataloging in Publication Data
Bloom, Christina
  Finding Your Soul Mate In The Faces of Love

  ISBN: 1-58244-225-8

  1. Relationships

Contents

Introduction

I was 32 when I separated from my husband. We were the best of friends but our romantic relationship was nonexistent. There just didn't seem to be any chemistry; there never was. Before our marriage, we were concerned about the absence of romantic compatibility; however, at the time, we believed that it existed only in fantasy and film. Neither of us had ever experienced it.

I later discovered that I was wrong. I learned that chemistry could be as strong as a potent drug. I realized that without romantic chemistry partners live like roommates who share a life without the "glue" that holds lovers together.

After my husband and I separated, I tortured myself trying to analyze what was responsible for the chemistry between two people. Where does it come from? Why do certain couples have it and others don't? I began to see something so obvious that it was thrilling. I noticed many couples who had similar facial features. It became apparent to me that perhaps they were attracted to the similarities in their mate's appearance. It was either the shape of their mouth, chin, cheeks, eyes, or overall facial structure. With more than one facial feature in common, the chemical compatibility seems to occur. In my own experience, I could be transported to heaven with just a look or a smile from his similar-featured face.

It makes perfect sense to me. What a way to assure the continuation of our species. It has been shown that odors are involved when people decide to mate. What is it that attracts people to one another's scent? What about a visual stimulus, liked a shared facial characteristic that arouses you when you see yourself in someone else?

My theory is not based on scientific research, but on both personal experience and extensive review of a myriad of photographs of celebrities and everyday people.

IN THE FACES OF L♥VE

(cont.)

When you look at the pictures in this book, keep an open mind and perhaps you will see what I see. If you are single, and you incorporate my theory into your quest for a mate, then search for your look-alike and I promise you sparks will fly!

This theory does not guarantee long-lasting love, but may steer you toward your soul mate. I believe that along with communication, compatibility, and of course, this magical chemistry, you will have found your life partner.

♥

Introduction

Acknowledgments

I would like to thank the people photographed. Without their unique pictures my theory would have been difficult to prove. Thank you to my parents Vincent and Marie Maneri who created my own physical features, which are similar to those of my mate. Also to my six sisters and their husbands who are my lifelong dear friends. I am very grateful to my two brothers and their wives for all their help.

I wish to thank my good friend, Roberta Schwartzman. Aside from her comic relief, her help with editing was greatly appreciated. Nancy Delahunt, my friend and ex-sister-in-law gave her input, which was valuable.

Thanks to my ex-husband, Peter Delahunt, who is my very supportive friend and who gave me unending advice for this project. Also, enormous thanks to my beautiful children, Pierce and Victoria who, from the beginning, helped me with my theory without question. My two stepchildren, Sara and Kate, also believed in my idea and were supportive.

In addition, thanks to my skeptical husband, David, who laughed at my theory, but joined me in my crusade and ultimately acknowledged the validity of this theory. I also thank you, David, for being my look-alike, my romantic partner, and initiating my interest in this project.

♥

Jennifer Aniston ♥ Brad Pitt

The striking similarity of this couple is the shapes of their faces and square chins. I imagine they have a strong bond and a strong chemistry!

Jennifer & Brad

Kelly & John

John Travolta ♥ Kelly Preston

These two are so cute together. What strikes me most is that their lips are the same exact shape! They both have high foreheads and eyes that are the same distance apart. It's no wonder that they fell in love . . .

IN THE FACES OF L♥VE

Denzel Washington ♥ Pauletta Washington

Pauletta & Denzel

I don't see the same shaped faces, but what I do see are the same noses, lips, and the same sized foreheads. Their eyes are the same distance apart and their chins seem similar. The similarities between these two are subtle but I see a match.

Lisa & Harry

Lisa Rinna ♥ Harry Hamlin

I was sad for Harry Hamlin when he separated from Nicolette Sheridan, but when I saw a picture of him and his current wife, Lisa Rinna, I knew that this match was meant to be! The shapes of their faces are identical, just look at their square jaws! I think what grabs me the most is their lips—so full and perfect for each other!

IN THE FACES OF L♥VE

Johnny Depp ♥ Vanessa Paradis

Vanessa & Johnny

This couple has a striking look. What is most noticeable to me are their heart-shaped faces. They also have small mouths that are full in the middle and taper toward the corners. Their resemblance is uncanny. I believe they are well matched.

Linda & Paul

Paul McCartney   Linda McCartney

This couple was so incredibly alike. No wonder their love was so intense. They truly found a soul mate in one another. Their faces were the same shapes; they both had round eyes; and their lips were almost identical.

Emma & Greg

Greg Chambury ♥ Emma Thompson

They both have a very down-to-earth sweetness about them. Observe the long faces and similarly spaced eyes. Note the thin upper and full lower lips on both. The distance between the bottom of the nose and the upper lip is the same. Maybe an easier way to contemplate my theory is to visualize superimposing her face on his and noticing the differences. I think there would be few discrepancies. These two look happy and well matched, and, I imagine are very compatible.

Julie & Bill

Julie Romanowski ♥ Bill Romanowski

These two could be brother and sister. Long faces and skinny lips are the most obvious similarities. Their eye shape and noses are also very much alike. The resemblance is so strong that my guess is that they are very compatible and will be together forever.

Sean Penn   Robin Wright Penn

♥

Robin & Sean

This couple also has similarly shaped faces and beautiful square chins. Their lips are similar in shape, their foreheads both high. If not for the rest of their lives, I think they will be together for a very long time.

Melanie & Antonio

Melanie Griffith ♥ Antonio Banderas

Chemistry, however, doesn't gurantee a happy relationship. I also believe that personality and lifestyle play a big part and in Hollywood, distractions become accentuated. In my opinion, these two could be in for a rough ride.

Ben Stiller ♥ Christine Taylor

Christine & Ben

I happen to think Ben Stiller is adorable!! What strikes me most about this couple are their deep-set eyes and long faces. Their lips are similar and they have high foreheads. A perfect pair!

Amy & Vince

Amy Grant ♥ Vince Gill

What is obvious to me about this couple is the fullness and the similarity of the shape of their faces. They both have high foreheads and matching lips.

I imagine this duo has the "glue" that will hold them together, even through difficult times. They will probably continue to have strong feelings for each other.

IN THE FACES OF L♥VE

Sophie Rhys Jones  Prince Edward

Sophie & Edward

A royal and facial match! They both have full lower and thin upper lips, long faces, and eyes that are closely spaced. I see a likeness that is apparent and in their case is hard to pinpoint but it is there . . .

By the way, Prince Charles and Camilla Parker Bowles's enduring relationship is, in my opinion, due to their strong facial similarities.

Heather & Paul

Heather Mills ♥ Paul McCartney

Paul revisited . . .

Luckily there is more than one person in the world to share your facial similarities... or life would be extremely lonely.

Can they be any more perfect for each other?

They both have the same shaped faces and the same square chins. Their noses are similar and I also see it in their eyes. To me, it is clear that they are matched flawlessly.

Valerie Bertinelli ♥ Eddie Van Halen

This super sweet couple recently split up, but their long romance is a testament to a facial feature match. They both have the same wide faces and their eyes are the same distance apart. It's difficult to tell but I believe their chins are square and their foreheads are the same height. Their similar heart-shaped faces provided them with a likeness that supported a twenty-year marriage in an arena that is almost impossible to maintain a marriage for any length of time.

Valerie & Eddie

Robin & Mike

Robin Ruzan ♥ Mike Myers

This funny man has made a total facial feature match. Wide faces and pointy chins are the most obvious but these two are also very similar in other ways. High foreheads and eyes the same distance apart make this couple's full faces so similar, therefore . . . a perfect match.

Gabrielle Reece ♥ Laird Reece

This athletic couple share a strong jaw line, well-defined cheekbones, deep-set eyes and prominent brows. They both have a full lower lip. The top of their upper lip (vermilion border) is the same distance from their nasal tip. If their physical compatibility is any reflection of their relationship these two are in it for the long haul.

Gabrielle & Laird

Leigh Anne & Brian

Brian Littrell ♥ Leigh Anne Littrell

This couple has a strong resemblance. They look like frightened deer in the headlights. The most striking characteristics are the eyes and noses. They have the same shape to their faces with high cheekbones.

They are so much alike, that I am almost in wonder. Can anyone doubt me?

Ava & Frank

Frank Sinatra ♥ Ava Gardner

They had chemistry and a very short but intense romance. Frank Sinatra was a man with many women in his life, but he was devastated when this relationship did not last. Where there's chemistry, there's pain. The similar features between this legendary duo are their shaped faces, eyes, and chins. My son brought to my attention the width of their smiles. This couple may have had chemistry, but their personalities were so strong that the longevity of the relationship was doomed.

Sheryl & Rob

Rob Lowe ♥ Sheryl Lowe

What tamed this actor? He had some growing up to do, but his facial feature match came into his life and the rest is history. He speaks so glowingly of her that I become a tad jealous when I read about them.

Their similarities are the same shaped faces and square chins. The eyes are the same distance apart on the face and the noses are similar in shape. They're perfect!

Tracy & Noah

Noah Wylie ♥ Tracy Warbin

Numerous friends and some family members were struck by this couples' strong similar facial features. Their eyes are the same distance apart and are similarly shaped. I also think that their noses are similar and their chins are square.

She's in the face business and he's an actor, but it doesn't matter when it comes to chemistry—it will happen to any two people who have a facial feature match.

IN THE FACES OF L♥VE

Gladys & Jean Claude

Jean Claude Van Damme ♥ Gladys Portuges

This couple has remarkable similarities. Most pronounced is the shape of their eyes, noses, and lips. The shapes of their faces, particularly their chins, are very similar.

It didn't surprise me when I heard they remarried. They had such strong chemistry that they bit the bullet and tried marriage a second time. They are a facial feature match in every way.

Davis Guggenheim ♥ Elizabeth Shue

The most striking similarities with this actress and her husband are their eyes and lips. Their eyes are wide on the face and their lips are similarly thin, the top lip even being thinner. Pay attention to the width of their smiles. I notice many couples having similar features but the women tend to have more delicate and smaller bone structure than the men. This couple is an example. She is a prettier and finer facial feature match to him!

Elizabeth & Davis

Everyday People

♥

Here are just a few couples I met and photographed. What do you think? Everywhere you look, there are couples who look similar to their partners. By being a little more aware, and observant of couples, you will see this phenomenon as much as I do.

And the Author? I think I would be remiss if I did not provide you with a picture of my spouse and me. In our youth we looked even more alike. You be the judge!

Christina & David

Conclusion

This list of couples with striking similarities could go on and on. The validity of my theory is not just proven by pictures of celebrities. Just look around you, at your family and friends, and will become obvious to you as it did to me.

In addition, let's take this one step further. Assuming that I am correct in my theory, let's go back to early man. If a man mates and reproduces with someone who resembles him, his offspring would also strongly resemble him. There would be no question of parentage. For a man who might be unsure of his mate, this would ease his insecurity and assure his territoriality. Again, for early man, a child who looked like both parents would enable the parents to bond to their offspring.

With this in mind, he or she who is single should pay close attention to facial features in a potential mate. If you find your look-alike, you may have found your soul mate. As my son points out, you don't fall in love with someone else, you fall in love with yourself . . .

♥